Conter

CW01455362

Would you like to get more out of this teaching?

Scan the QR code to access this teaching in video or audio formats to help you dive even deeper as you study.

Accessing the teaching this way will help you get even more out of this booklet.

awmi.net/browse

GRACE
The Power of
The Gospel

Andrew Wommack

Published by Andrew Wommack Ministries, Inc.

Woodland Park, CO 80863

ISBN 13 TP: 978-1-59548-779-7

For Worldwide Distribution, Printed in the USA

1 2 3 4 5 6 / 28 27 26 25

Introduction

The Gospel is the most basic, foundational message of the New Testament, yet it's probably the most misunderstood. Today, many churches operate according to a religious system that does not preach the same Gospel that the Apostle Paul did. They mix it with the Law, which isn't the Gospel at all.

Do you struggle with feelings of condemnation or guilt? Are you constantly evaluating your relationship with God according to your performance? Do you want to see more of God's power operating in your life? All these things are related to how you understand the Gospel.

The book of Romans was written to explain the Gospel so that anybody could understand it. But some things are so simple that you need help to misunderstand them. And, sad to say, we've had a lot of help misunderstanding the simplicity of the Gospel!

Many people have been taught (as I once was) that you have to do something to earn God's goodness—that everything is about your performance. That is a religious mindset. There are many people today who wouldn't consider themselves to be religious, but their error on this one issue shows they really are.

They base their hope of entering heaven on going to church, performing rituals, trying to live up to a standard of morality, or some other thing. They are trying to earn what God has already given as a gift.

You see, the Gospel is the power of God (Rom. 1:16), and that power is found in His grace. Verses like Acts 20:24 and Galatians 1:6 both use the terms "*Gospel*" and "*grace*" interchangeably. So, when you understand the Gospel—or the grace of God—it will release the power of God into your life.

When you truly get a hold of the grace of God, it sets you free *from* sin, not free *to* sin. You'll wind up living holier accidentally than you ever would on purpose. You'll serve God out of love more than you ever would out of legalism.

It takes a supernatural revelation by the Holy Spirit to be able to understand these things. But once you do, it'll transform the way that you *recognize* God, the way that you *relate* to God, and the way that you *receive* from God.

Relationship vs. Religion

Shortly after I had a miraculous encounter with the Lord in 1968, I was at a meeting and heard a man say that if a person could understand the Apostle Paul's letter to the Romans, it would transform their life. And I took that as a challenge.

I started studying the book of Romans, and I struggled with it for years. That's because I was raised in a legalistic, performance-based religion. As a result, I was living a life holier than most people ever thought about living, thinking it would please God. I was trusting in my holiness, and that blinded me to receiving from the Lord by grace.

I got born again when I was eight years old, but by the time I was eighteen, I had become a religious Pharisee. I never used profanity when I spoke. I never smoked a cigarette. I never touched a drop of liquor. I didn't even drink coffee. You may be thinking, *Coffee?* Well, you have a scripture to stand on for drinking coffee. Mark 16:18 says that if believers "*drink any deadly thing, it shall not hurt them.*"

I even started a special youth visitation program on Tuesdays where the young people of the church would go door to door, sharing the Gospel, and getting people to repeat "The Sinner's Prayer." I couldn't wait to submit my report every week to show how many converts I had made so that I could get a pat on the back.

Then, on March 23, 1968, the Lord showed up at a Saturday night prayer meeting, and I saw the glory of God. I didn't see it with my physical eyes, but it came by revelation. And compared to the glory and holiness of God, all of my self-righteousness was like filthy rags (Is. 64:6). I won't go into all the details here, but I have a booklet titled *My Appointment with God*, where I share about this miraculous encounter with the Lord and the revelation of His love and grace that changed my life.

The book of Romans is Paul's masterpiece on the grace of God, which is completely contrary to performance-based religion. Jesus said in Mark 7:13 that the traditions and doctrines of men make the Word of God *"of none effect."* Paul's teaching on the grace of God and our liberty in Jesus Christ was so different than what I'd been taught that my traditions and the doctrines of men were canceling out the great truths of the book of Romans.

I just kept studying and started getting revelation—and I'm still getting revelation. It's not like I've got everything figured out. But I have come to a place where Romans is one of my favorite books of the Bible. It's just powerful. And if you understand the book of Romans, you can't help but fall in love with God for the great things He's done and how He relates to you through grace.

The Good News

For the wages of sin is death; but the gift of God is eternal life through Jesus Christ our Lord.

Romans 6:23

Today, most Christians think the word "Gospel" is just a word that identifies religious things. But religion only focuses on the first part of this verse—*"For the wages of sin is death."* Religious people preach their hearts out about hellfire and damnation. There is a place for that, but if God's wrath and judgment are all that's presented, it's not the Gospel.

It's been said that the word "Gospel" is translated from a Greek word that was seldom ever used. That's because it was only used to describe something so awesome that it seemed unrealistic or nearly too good to be true. *Nothing on earth* was nearly too good to be true. But the life, death, and resurrection of Jesus changed all that! Contrary to what is traditionally taught, the Gospel doesn't merely mean "good news." It is better understood to mean "nearly-too-good-to-be-true news."

Years ago, I used to give out tracts to people on the streets. They were little pamphlets that Christians would use to start conversations with nonbelievers and hopefully get them to accept Jesus as Lord. We used tracts that said things like, "Repent or else!" or "Turn or burn!"

We had another tract called "What Must I Do to Go to Hell?" And when the person opened it up, it was completely blank inside. There was nothing in there. That prompted the Christian to say to the nonbeliever, "That's right! You don't have to do anything. You're already a sinner. You're headed to hell!"

I know those things sound really strong, but we thought that was "the Gospel." I was modeling things the way I had been taught. We actually sat under a preacher who would scream and yell. He'd jump on top of the pulpit where a minister would normally put their Bible, bend over, grab the microphone, and just scream things like, "You're going to *hellllll*!"

People may think I'm making it up, but those things really happened. Ministers would scream and yell all these things, and then they'd say, "That's the Gospel!" It's true that people who don't accept the sacrifice of Jesus will spend an eternity in hell, but that's not good news. And it's certainly not nearly-too-good-to-be-true news.

The Gospel is the good news that, despite our sins and the judgment we deserve, God has provided complete redemption for us (Eph. 1:7). Even more specifically, the word "Gospel" describes the grace that enables us to receive this forgiveness.

We aren't called to convict people of their sins. We're called to convince them that the only way to obtain righteousness, or right standing, with God is by putting faith in what Jesus did for them, and not in their own works (Gal. 2:16).

The Grace of God

I marvel that ye are so soon removed from him that called you into the grace of Christ unto another Gospel.

Galatians 1:6

Paul used the terms "Gospel" and "grace" interchangeably in Galatians 1:6, quoted above. Notice how "*the grace of Christ*" clearly implies the Gospel.

The Gospel isn't only the belief that there is salvation; it's also the specific method by which salvation is obtained: grace. That means the religious way of thinking—if you act good and do good, then you'll be good—isn't the true Gospel.

The word "grace" can be understood to mean unmerited, unearned, and undeserved favor. Therefore, the good news is that grace has nothing to do with you (Eph. 2:8). Salvation, however, is not dependent on grace alone. If it were, everyone would be saved and going to heaven because God's grace is the same toward everyone (Titus 2:11). He has already given the gift of salvation to everyone through Jesus. But it must be received by each individual through faith.

The Gospel is directly related to the grace of God. That's the only way forgiveness of sin can be obtained. It isn't through our holiness or good works. God isn't looking for the "good" people to save because there are none (Ps. 14:3; Rom. 3:10; and 23). Therefore, He justifies (or extends salvation toward) the ungodly (Rom. 4:5).

The Gospel is God's gift of eternal life through Jesus Christ our Lord. The good news is that God doesn't want to send anyone to hell (2 Pet. 3:9). You don't have to go through a tremendous amount of religious instruction or observance to receive it (though being a disciple of the Word will help you better understand it). Salvation is a gift.

Grace is what sets true Christianity apart from every other religion. Other religions may agree that Jesus existed and that His teachings are admirable. They say He was a good man and maybe even a prophet, but definitely not God manifest in the flesh. They refuse to acknowledge Jesus Christ as the only way to salvation or a right relationship with God.

Every false religion—even religious Christianity—puts the burden of salvation on the individual. In other words, their version of salvation is based upon your performance. If you live holy enough, do enough good things, and observe all of the rituals and rules, then you might be able to be saved. The problem is—and Paul makes this crystal clear—that none of us can live up to those standards.

For all have sinned, and come short of the glory of God.

Romans 3:23

All you must do is believe and receive. Believe what Jesus has done through His death, burial, and resurrection, and receive cleansing from all your sins and the freedom and liberty it brings. That's the Gospel!

No Other Gospel

To all that be in Rome, beloved of God, called to be saints: Grace to you and peace from God our Father, and the Lord Jesus Christ.

Romans 1:7

In the early church, many born-again Jews believed Christianity was just an extension of the Old Testament. They considered all of the basic tenets of their religion—the Law, dietary regulations, circumcision, and other rituals—to be the foundation of their faith in Christ. They were trying to mix the Old Covenant with the New.

To counter these things, the Apostle Paul wrote a letter to the Christians in Rome. They were mostly Gentiles who had received the Gospel, been born again, and were committed to following Jesus as Lord. But they were being troubled by those who were trying to mix legalism with Christianity—the Judaizers.

Before he was born again, Paul was very legalistic, even to the point of persecuting Christians. But then, Jesus met him on the road to Damascus, and his life was radically transformed (Acts 9:1-6). He then spent three years in the deserts of Arabia, trying to rearrange his thinking (Gal. 1:18) and reconciling grace with what he knew about the Law. So, when he saw the Judaizers trying to drag Christians back into performance-based religion, the gloves came off.

In his letter to the Galatians, Paul starts by saying, "If anyone preaches any other gospel than what I preached, let them be accursed" (Gal. 1:8). He called the Galatians "*foolish*" and "*bewitched*" (Gal. 3:1) for falling back into legalism. He told them that if they trusted in things like circumcision for salvation (Gal. 5:3-4), they had fallen from grace. Those are some strong statements.

Whoever wrote the letter to the Hebrews (I tend to believe it was Paul, though he's never mentioned by name) also dealt with these same things. Written specifically to people with a religious mindset, Hebrews encourages them to embrace faith in the finished work of Christ. Throughout the letter, the writer uses Jewish tradition (the Old Testament patriarchs, tabernacle, priesthood, and sacrificial systems) to show how Jesus perfectly fulfilled the Law.

The book of Romans covers much of the same material, but Paul presents things doctrinally—in a systematic way. Paul shows believers how they no longer have to earn the favor of God. It is a gift. The purpose of the Law wasn't to set us free but rather to show us our need for a Savior and drive us to Him.

This revelation is foundational for maintaining a close and living relationship with God. You see, a person might do good for a while, but all have sinned and fallen short of God's glory (Rom. 3:23). That's why we need a Savior! We must constantly place our faith in God's goodness, not our own. That way, when we fall short, we will run to God and not away from Him.

A Religious Mindset

For I am not ashamed of the Gospel of Christ: for it is the power of God unto salvation to every one that believeth; to the Jew first, and also to the Greek.

Romans 1:16

Paul constantly encountered the religious mindset. The Jews of his day were so legalistic that they had a limit on how many steps you could take on a Sabbath Day. One group, the Essenes, had it in their writings that you couldn't even have a bowel movement on the Sabbath. It was oppressive!

These people had such strict religious practices that it makes you wonder how anyone could live under them. Then Paul came along, saying he was not ashamed of the nearly-too-good-to-be-true news that Jesus paid for everything.

Relationship with God was no longer based on a person's performance. I'm sure you can see how this challenged the religious minds of his day.

Today, it may not be as bad as it was with the scribes and Pharisees, but the principles are the same. Religion teaches that you have to keep all of the rules and regulations to be accepted by God. But that kind of thinking will actually stop you from experiencing the power of God in your life.

In my meetings, I'll often give the testimony of how I saw my son raised from the dead. Then, I'll ask, "If somebody were to fall over dead here today, how many of you believe that God can raise him from the dead?" People all over the room will raise their hands and start shouting "Amen!"

Generally, the people who come to my meetings are Spirit-filled people. They believe in the power of God and that miracles happen today. So, I can typically get nearly 100 percent of them excited about raising the dead. But then I'll ask, "How many of you would come up here and pray for that person?"

All of a sudden, people's faith turns into fear. Their excitement turns to dread. Is that because they quit believing that God can raise the dead or do miracles today? No! They still believe it can happen. They just don't believe He would do it through them.

That is because many Christians still live with a sin consciousness. They live with a sense of unworthiness. In some cases, people have been taught that if they die with unconfessed sins—even after being born again—they'll go straight to hell! In a sense, they think they have to be born again *again* every time they sin. But that's not what the Bible teaches. We have been sanctified and perfected forever through Jesus' sacrifice, once and for all (Heb. 10:10, 14; and Rom. 4:8).

If what I'm saying describes you, then you are living under the Law. It makes you live in a constant state of condemnation, knowing that God can do something but doubting that He will do it for *you* because of your unworthiness.

Why Live Holy?

Many people are not experiencing the goodness of God in their lives. And it's not because they don't believe He can do something. They are just trying to earn it. Their conscience condemns them and keeps them from believing they'll receive freely. Why? Because they think they aren't worthy enough.

When a person has been grounded in that kind of thinking, and someone comes along and tells them they can receive from God regardless of performance, it's offensive to them. Religious people may respond, "So, you're saying that all of my good works and the fact that I haven't done all these bad things don't make me any closer to God?" But that's exactly what Paul was saying—everything we receive from God comes through what Jesus *already* did.

I've had people come to me for prayer and say things like, "I just can't understand. I fast, I pray, I study the Word, I go to church, and I pay my tithes. Why hasn't God healed me?" Without realizing it, they told me exactly why they hadn't experienced what they desired from the Lord.

A person like that isn't looking at what Jesus did for them. Instead, they are relying on what they did for Jesus. They are trusting in their own holiness, thinking they are such a good person and, therefore, deserve something from God. That approach is the very thing that stops them from receiving.

All of your self-denial, going to church, reading the Bible, and other good works won't make God love you more. Living a holy lifestyle actually makes *you* love God more. It will draw *you* closer to Him, not the other way around.

Now, there are other reasons for you to live holy. That's because sin will give Satan inroad to your life. You become his servant (Rom. 6:16), and he is not out to bless you. Satan is the author of sin, and if you yield to it, he is just going to steal, kill, and destroy (John 10:10). If you give him an opportunity, the devil will eat your lunch and pop the bag!

It's said that mercy is getting what you don't deserve, and justice is getting what you do deserve. That means God loves you independent of what you deserve. Justice was served through Jesus. But that doesn't free you up to just go out and live however you want. Even though God loves you, there are still earthly consequences to your actions.

For instance, you could misapply this revelation and say, "If it doesn't matter what I do, I think I'll go rob a bank." God will still love you, but when you get caught, tried, and sentenced, you'll be experiencing His love in a prison cell. Yes, you can have a wonderful time in fellowship with the Lord by grace through faith, but you're still going to experience the consequences of your actions. So, living holy is the better deal.

An Intuitive Knowledge of God

For the wrath of God is revealed from heaven against all ungodliness and unrighteousness of men, who hold the truth in unrighteousness; because that which may be known of God is manifest in them; for God hath shewed it *unto them. For the invisible things of him from the creation of the world are clearly seen, being understood by the things that are made,* even *his eternal power and Godhead; so that they are without excuse.*

Romans 1:18–20

One of the reasons why constantly preaching about hellfire and damnation is counterintuitive to the Gospel of grace is that each individual already has an intuitive knowledge of God's wrath against *"all ungodliness and unrighteousness of men."*

Even the people who have lived in the most remote parts of the earth and have never heard the Gospel will be accountable to God someday in eternity. Why? Because they had this intuitive knowledge that there is a God, they're separated from Him, and they need salvation. They'll be *"without excuse."*

I saw this truth vividly illustrated as a soldier in Vietnam. Near my brigade headquarters were three ancient temples standing side by side. Since there was only about a foot between them, they looked like one large temple. At the time, trees were growing out of them, and parts of the buildings were crumbling because of the weather and lack of use.

17

When I asked about them, someone told me that these temples predated Christianity in Vietnam by at least 500 years. However, the people of that time worshiped a god that was manifest in three persons. These things relate to what Christianity calls the Trinity. I'm not saying that these people worshiped the true God or that they had a true revelation of Him. But this does show an intuitive knowledge of the Godhead.

Many of my fellow soldiers professed to be atheists. They tried to deny the intuitive knowledge in their hearts that there was a God, and they were sinners. One guy even walked in on one of my Bible studies and started throwing a bunch of intellectual questions at me that I couldn't answer.

While he was grilling me, I kept saying, "I don't know the answers to all of these questions, but I know in my heart that God is real." By the time he left, taking all the people in my Bible study with him, I was speechless. But it wasn't long before that guy returned and said, "I want what you've got." And all I could think was, *You do?*

He recognized that I didn't waver in my conviction because I had a personal relationship with the Lord. I had received the Gospel as a gift, acting on the intuitive knowledge of God that was already in me. And I got to lead that man to Jesus!

Sin Came Alive

Now we know that what things soever the law saith,
it saith to them who are under the law: that every
mouth may be stopped, and all the world may become
guilty before God. Therefore by the deeds of the law
there shall no flesh be justified in his sight: for by the
law is *the knowledge of sin.*

Romans 3:19–20

Some people think that the law was given for everyone. But the Law was given as part of the covenant between God and the Jews. The law was never intended for the Gentiles. In the Early Church, Jewish Christians were saying that Gentile believers had to convert to Judaism and observe all of the laws before they could become Christians. But Paul said the Law wasn't given to the Gentiles (Rom. 2:14).

The Law was never given for the purpose of justification. The Law wasn't even given to produce salvation or the forgiveness of sins. According to Paul, the purpose of the Law is to shut our mouths. In other words, the Law removes all of our excuses and comparisons. It makes us aware of our sinful nature and renders us guilty before God.

The Law revived the sin on the inside of us and gave it an opportunity against us. The Law didn't strengthen us in our battle against sin (Rom. 7:7–11). It strengthened sin in its battle against us (1 Cor. 15:56). Most people think the Law was given to break sin's dominion over us. But that's not so.

Simply put, sin had already defeated mankind. Even if we kept ninety-nine out of a hundred commandments, the one we broke would cause us to become guilty of everything (James 2:10). In God's eyes, even the slightest sin contaminates us.

God doesn't grade on a curve. He doesn't change the standard of the Law to make up for our poor performance. It's all or nothing. Those who are trying to overcome sin are fighting a losing battle because all have already sinned and fallen short of the glory of God (Rom. 3:23).

Through Jesus, the righteousness of God is available without keeping the Law. In other words, you can become righteous, enjoy right standing with God—just as if you'd never sinned—and be completely forgiven, made clean and pure in God's sight, without keeping the law. This upsets religious people.

The entire Old Testament—the Law and the Prophets— pointed forward to this (Rom. 3:21). It foreshadowed and prophesied it. People who take commandments in the Old Testament Law and teach that you must do them to be accepted by God totally misunderstand its purpose. The Law and the Prophets testify to the coming of the Righteous One—the Lord Jesus Christ—and righteousness given as a free gift through faith in His name.

Peace with God

Therefore being justified by faith, we have peace with God through our Lord Jesus Christ.

Romans 5:1

Paul was saying that the only way to have peace with God is to be justified—made righteous—by faith, not by works or performance. We take for granted today that many things in the Law are no longer religiously observed, such as circumcision and sacrifices.

All the same, some still believe that God justified Abraham because of his holy life, but that isn't true. God promised Abraham that offspring would come from his own body, and they would become as numerous as the stars in the sky and the dust of the earth. In him, all the nations of the earth would be blessed (Gen. 12:2–3; 13:16; and 15:4–5).

Abraham *believed* God's promises, and the Lord counted him righteous (Gen. 15:6 and Rom. 4:2–5). Abraham became righteous *by faith* thirteen years before he received the sign of righteousness—circumcision (Rom. 4:9–11). So, he was *already* righteous before being circumcised.

Now, Abraham's performance *did* cost him in the natural realm. Lying to kings about his wife caused him hardship (Gen. 12:11–18 and 20:1–2). And going to Sarah's maid and getting her pregnant certainly caused him some grief (Gen. 16:3–4). But God didn't relate to Abraham based on his holiness. If He had, Abraham would've been in serious trouble!

While repenting over his sin with Bathsheba (2 Sam. 11), David said that God didn't desire sacrifice (Ps. 51:16). That was a radical statement for David's day. The Law prescribed certain sacrifices to be offered for the sin he committed. However, according to Scripture, David didn't offer those sacrifices.

David simply repented before God with the knowledge that this was what the Lord was truly after (Ps. 51:17). He had a revelation that the Old Testament Law contained types and shadows of the Savior to come. David knew that the real thing God was after was his heart.

This shows that it's not any of the things we do that make us righteous. It's not water baptism, the Lord's Supper, or our own personal holiness. Those things are byproducts of our relationship with God. They're the fruit of being in right standing with Him, not the root of it.

I've dealt with many people who have argued with me, saying things like, "You've got to be holy and do all these things to have God accept you." I've found that people who believe and preach that do not have real peace in their lives. The only way I have encountered real peace in my heart is through understanding that salvation is a gift and that I am justified by faith.

Saved by Grace

But God commendeth his love toward us, in that, while we were yet sinners, Christ died for us. Much more then, being now justified by his blood, we shall be saved from wrath through him. For if, when we were enemies, we were reconciled to God by the death of his Son, much more, being reconciled, we shall be saved by his life.

Romans 5:8–10

The first part of this is often taken out of context to make the point that God loves the sinner. That is a true statement, but it is not the point that Paul was making.

In context, Paul was talking to Christians about the grace of God. He was making a comparison. He used the truth about God commending His love toward us while we were still sinners as a step to another truth. Not viewing this verse in context has caused many people to accept salvation by grace but then go back under the deception that they have to live "good enough" for God to use them as Christians.

While realizing one truth, they completely missed the whole point of what Paul was saying. These verses, taken in context, conclusively prove that we begin and continue our walk with God through faith in His grace (Col. 2:6).

Since religion preaches a performance-based relationship with God instead of preaching the Gospel, most people believe that the Lord loves them when they were sinners, but He gets harder on them once they're saved.

Think about what would happen if an unbeliever came into a church service drunk. Most Christians would go up to them and start ministering God's love, mercy, and grace, saying, "Jesus loves you and died for your sins. He wants to forgive you and change your life." They would minister the Gospel based on God's grace, not that person's past performance.

But if that person got born again and came back the next week drunk again, those same people who ministered grace, forgiveness, and mercy would turn around and say, "If you don't straighten up, God is going to get you. Change your ways, or the wrath of God will come on you!"

How much did you read the Bible before you were born again? How much had you fasted and prayed before you were saved? How faithful were you in paying your tithes? The answer for nearly everyone is that they weren't faithful in any of these areas. You were just a rank sinner, but you believed the Gospel! That's what changed things.

You are not only saved by grace, but you also maintain your relationship with God by grace. This means you are healed by grace, delivered by grace, and prospered by grace. None of the benefits of salvation come to you based on your performance.

Sin Nature

Wherefore, as by one man sin entered into the world, and death by sin; and so death passed upon all men, for that all have sinned.

Romans 5:12

Through Adam, we all became sinners. It wasn't our individual actions of sin that made us sinners, but the propensity for sin that we inherited—the sin nature. We were born with a sin nature. That's what makes us commit individual actions of sin.

You see, before you were born again, you may have done some good things. But you consistently lived as a sinner because that was your true nature. You were enslaved to sin yet set free from that enslavement through salvation! It's not something you work at. It's not given to you based on your performance.

For by grace are ye saved through faith; and that not of yourselves: it is *the gift of God: not of works, lest any man should boast.*

Ephesians 2:8–9

Through Adam's fall, sin passed on to everybody (Rom. 5:15). You didn't do anything to become a sinner. You were born into it (Ps. 51:5). But when you receive salvation, you are born again into righteousness. You don't do anything to earn it. You receive it as a free gift (Rom. 5:16).

When you get born again, God puts His nature on the inside of you. If you renew your mind (Rom. 12:2), this new nature will help you to live a holy life. The only thing you must do to access this grace is to have faith in what Jesus did for you (Rom. 5:1–2).

Back in the late 1960s, a friend of mine started telling me about these things and invited me to a Bible study. I was still in a denominational church at the time and steeped in the religious teaching I grew up with. So, when I walked in the door, I immediately became offended.

A woman was leading that Bible study! According to my church, women were not supposed to teach adults about the Bible. Also, there were long-haired hippies in attendance. Our church taught that if a man's hair touched the collar of his shirt, he went straight to hell!

Then they started talking about being righteous. I thought they would admit that they were still sinners, but they didn't. They proclaimed they were righteous in Christ.

So, I countered with, "*All have sinned, and come short of the glory of God*" (Rom. 3:23), "*There is none righteous, no, not one*" (Rom. 3:10), and "*All our righteousnesses are as filthy rags*" (Is. 64:6). I gave it to them with both barrels!

Instead of getting angry, they just continued to walk in love. For every one scripture I quoted, they quoted three or four about them being righteous. It just overwhelmed me! So, I determined that I would study things for myself. After about a week of poring over the Word, I learned that I was righteous as a gift and not through what I did.

'Shall We Continue in Sin?'

What shall we say then? Shall we continue in sin, that grace may abound? God forbid. How shall we, that are dead to sin, live any longer therein?

Romans 6:1–2

The Law was what made sin reign unto death. Empowered by the Law, sin brought forth death (Rom. 6:23). We were also dominated by condemnation and guilt. But now that we're in Christ and under the New Covenant, "*grace reign*[s] *through righteousness unto eternal life*" (Rom. 5:21). Instead of the Law, grace is now the dominant factor.

So, if we are understanding and sharing the Gospel correctly, someone will inevitably ask, "Are you saying that I can just go live in sin?" Paul's answer to this was a resounding "No!"

He began to answer this question by saying, "*God forbid.*" This was the strongest renunciation Paul could have made in the Greek language without employing some type of profanity. This was an emphatic, absolute denial. He was saying, "No! Absolutely not! Let it never be!" Paul was not encouraging sin in any way. And neither are you when you are ministering the Gospel of grace.

The primary reason why Christians shouldn't live in sin is because they are no longer, by nature, children of the devil. After being born again, a person no longer has a sinful nature but a new nature (Rom. 6:6 and 2 Cor. 5:17). The second reason to live holy is that it will stop Satan's inroads into your life (Rom. 6:16).

Your motive for living holy is not to get God to accept you. If you are a born-again believer, you live holy because it's in your nature to live that way, and you don't want to give the devil any access into your life.

Living holy is a fruit—not a root—of salvation. It's a by-product of living in right relationship with God, but not a means to obtain it. For example, if you never studied the Word again, God would love you exactly the same. But *you* wouldn't love God the same because you wouldn't have the revelation of His truth (John 8:32 and 17:17).

If you're truly born again, it's in your new nature to hunger for the truth. We're in a battle, and Satan is coming against us. So, it's to our advantage to get into the Word because it changes our hearts and corrects our attitudes. Being in God's Word gives us revelation and helps keep the devil from having access into our lives.

The Old Man Is Dead

Knowing this, that our old man is crucified with [Christ], *that the body of sin might be destroyed, that henceforth we should not serve sin. For he that is dead is freed from sin.*

Romans 6:6–7

Born-again believers do not have a sinful nature—*the "old man"*—any longer. You need to understand that when you were born again, your spirit instantly became righteous

(2 Cor. 5:17 and Heb. 12:23). You've been set free from the power of sin!

Before we are born again, our sin nature leads us to commit acts of sin. Even if somehow we could deal with our actions and restrain the amount of sin we commit, there's still no human way to deal with the sin nature.

A person can't just change their nature simply by decreasing their actions of sin! But when we are born again, the old sin nature is crucified, dead, and buried. Believers are born again with a brand-new, righteous nature. The old nature that expressed itself through sin is gone. A new nature, which desires to express itself through holy living, has now taken its place.

Believers are placed into the body of Christ when they are born again. When that happens, they are baptized into Jesus' death (Rom. 6:3). This makes the things that He died to accomplish a reality in a person's life (Rom. 6:4–6). In other words, every believer has participated in the death of their old nature (old man) through Jesus. Christians are now dead to sin.

It's important to understand that Paul was talking about sin (the sin nature), not sins (individual actions). Through

Jesus Christ, God went to the very root of sin—our sin nature—and dealt with it.

God didn't only give us the ability to overcome actions of sin, but He dealt with the part of us that was corrupted and forcing us to live in sin. When Jesus went to the cross, He became sin so we could become the righteousness of God (2 Cor. 5:21). That means the Christian doesn't live a changed life (changed behaviors), but rather an exchanged life (with a new nature).

Jesus only died unto sin once, and you only die unto that old sin nature one time. The Bible says your old man is dead, and it does not resurrect every morning. If you really understood that it's not your nature to live in sin anymore, you would be free from sin.

Created Righteous

For they being ignorant of God's righteousness, and going about to establish their own righteousness, have not submitted themselves unto the righteousness of God. For Christ is the end of the law for righteousness to every one that believeth.

Romans 10:3–4

You don't become righteous through your own actions—you are created righteous (2 Cor. 5:17). When you were born again, God gave you a righteous nature. But the sad thing is that most Christians are ignorant of this. They don't know their born-again spirit is righteous. They aren't aware of the truth that righteousness comes as a gift from God. So, they try to maintain righteousness based on actions, which can never be the basis of our relationship with God.

There are two types of righteousness—God's righteousness and our own righteousness (Rom. 10:3). They are mutually exclusive. You can't trust in the gift of righteousness through Christ while also trusting in self-righteousness. You can't be self-dependent and God-dependent simultaneously.

You're either trusting God's grace or your works for salvation, but not a combination of the two. Therefore, if you're trying to establish your own righteousness as the foundation of your relationship with God, then you haven't submitted to His righteousness. God's grace, mercy, and opinion toward you are not based on your actions. They're totally unmerited and completely unearned.

For believers, the Law has fulfilled its purpose (Rom. 10:4). It's no longer a way we pursue righteousness. In truth, the Law was never given to produce right standing with God.

It was given to show us how completely separated from Him we were.

The Law was given to make the old sin nature rise up on the inside of us and overcome us. It was given to reveal to us our need for a Savior. When we turn from self-righteousness, place our faith in Christ for salvation, and receive God's free gift of grace, the Law then has accomplished what it was given to do.

Jesus came and fulfilled every precept of the Law (Matt. 5:17). As a result, He literally earned right standing with God. He already had it by His very nature, and then He also obtained it through His actions. Therefore, Jesus had it by inheritance and by conquest. He obtained right standing with God through every means available.

By fulfilling the Law, Jesus brings salvation to everyone who puts faith in Him. We receive what Jesus deserved because He took what we deserved (2 Cor. 5:21).

Renew Your Mind

And be not conformed to this world: but be ye transformed by the renewing of your mind, that ye may

prove what is *that good, and acceptable, and perfect,*
will of God.

Romans 12:2

The word "*transformed*" here is the Greek word *meta-morphoo*.[1] It's where we get the word "metamorphosis." It relates to how a caterpillar spins a cocoon and transforms into a butterfly. If you want to see your life truly transformed, the way it happens is through the renewing of your mind.

The key to living the Christian life is the renewing of the mind. You are a three-part being: spirit, soul, and body (1 Thess. 5:23). When you were born again, your spirit changed—but your mind didn't. It remained unrenewed.

Everything you need is already in your born-again spirit—the life of God, the faith of God, the joy of God, the peace of God, the anointing of God, and everything else that's of God—but it's only going to manifest itself in your life to the degree you renew your mind.

If you think that you're "just an old sinner saved by grace" (as religious people often say) and that it's only a matter of time before the sin nature drives you to do something wrong, you're believing something contrary to Scripture.

When someone's spirit leaves their body, that's death (James 2:26). Although that spirit goes to be with the Lord, it leaves behind a body. For a brief period of time, that body doesn't decay but still looks like the person who once lived in it. As a matter of fact, a dead body can still have some reactions.

A friend of mine worked in the morgue on the thirteenth floor of Parkland Hospital in Dallas, Texas. One time, he put a corpse on a slab and then turned around to get something. When he looked back, the body had sat up with its eyes and mouth wide open. It was just sitting there with its arms dangling at its side. My friend nearly jumped out of the window!

He thought this guy was alive, and it scared him. So, he ran and got somebody. They came back in, checked it out, and pushed the body back down onto the slab. Even though this guy was dead, electrical impulses were causing his body to twitch and move. He was totally dead, but his body still acted like it was alive.

If you acknowledge the truth that the sin nature's hold on you has been broken, and you are now dead to sin, all you're dealing with now is *the body of sin* (Rom. 6:6). It's not the actual sin nature itself, but the body it left behind.

The next step is to destroy that body of sin by systematically tearing down wrong thoughts with the Word of God, replacing them with godly thoughts so *"we should not serve sin"* (Rom. 6:6).

Weak in Him

O wretched man that I am! who shall deliver me from the body of this death? I thank God through Jesus Christ our Lord. So then with the mind I myself serve the law of God; but with the flesh the law of sin.

Romans 7:24–25

The Christian life isn't just hard to live—it's impossible! It's humanly impossible to love your neighbor as you love yourself. But because God commanded us to do it, people will try—and fail!

When someone spits on you or slaps your face, it's humanly impossible to turn the other cheek (Matt. 5:39). You can't do that in your flesh. You don't have the natural ability to pray for those who despitefully use you or do good to those who hate you (Matt. 5:44). You just can't do those things naturally.

Your flesh must be crucified so that Christ can live through you (Gal. 2:20). You must learn to totally deny yourself, have no confidence in the flesh (Phil. 3:3), and constantly become more dependent on Him.

For instance, in their flesh, some might grit their teeth and say, "I'm going to love this person!" But you, through your born-again spirit, can pray, "Father, I choose to deny myself and let You love them through me." You can just let God's love flow out of your spirit rather than do something impossible out of your flesh (Matt. 19:26).

For example, I just read about a man who spent thirty-six years in prison for killing his wife, but he was innocent. While he was in prison, he turned to the Lord and actually became a pastor to other inmates. God did such a wonderful work in his life that when the real murderer of his wife confessed, he thanked him for doing what was right by finally telling the truth, and said he was praying for him that this would be the start of him following the Lord for the rest of his life.

That's not normal. That reflects a heart that has been changed by the supernatural power of God. Only a person who has experienced forgiveness can turn around and forgive others like that. That kind of forgiveness is beyond our human ability. It's the work of God in our lives.

Not enough Christians have experienced the consistent life of Jesus flowing through them. Too many believers are busy trying to live *for* Jesus instead of letting Him live *through* them. People will do their best until they come to the end of their own human ability and then cry out to God for help. That's why people get into so many problems.

It's not a matter of doing your own thing and then asking God to bless it. That's the wrong attitude. You should say, "Father, what's Your will for me? I don't have any agenda of my own." When you reach that place where you let Him tell you what He wants you to do, it won't be you doing it any longer. It will be the Lord working through you.

Years ago, I called a woman on the telephone and asked, "How are you doing?" She answered, "I'm weak in Him." At first, I wondered, *What does that mean?* You see, a lot of people will say religious-sounding things to project a false humility. But after we hung up and I pondered it some more, I thought, *That's pretty good!*

This woman was saying, "I'm learning how not to trust in myself but to recognize my weakness and let Jesus live through me." Instead of doing her own thing and then turning to God when she got in trouble, she was learning how to deny herself and just do what God was leading her to do.

No Condemnation

There is therefore now no condemnation to them which are in Christ Jesus, who walk not after the flesh, but after the Spirit. For the law of the Spirit of life in Christ Jesus hath made me free from the law of sin and death.

Romans 8:1–2

If you'll let your born-again spirit live through you, there is no condemnation, judgment, or sentence against you. Nothing can stop you. Nothing can hold you down. Your born-again man doesn't have any limitations or inadequacies. As Jesus is right now, so are you in your spirit (1 Cor. 6:17 and 1 John 4:17).

The word "condemn" is sometimes used to refer to a building that is "unfit for use."[2] In a sense, when a person experiences shame, guilt, and lack of confidence due to sin, they feel unfit for God's use. The devil does that by saying to someone, "You worthless thing. What makes you think God would use you?"

The Law that governed the old man—that old sin nature—declared, "You're a failure. You can't lay hands on the sick and see them recover. You can't prosper. You can't be happy. You can't have joy." But that old man is dead and gone for the one who is in Christ.

The Law that enforced sin's rule over a person's life doesn't rule over them once they are born again (Rom. 8:2). Because we were imperfect through our flesh, the Old Testament Law—instead of being something good—became our condemnation. So, God sent His own Son as a man and judged sin in His flesh (Rom. 8:3).

There's a difference between the concepts of "in the flesh" and "after the flesh," and "in the Spirit" and "after the Spirit" (Rom. 8:4–5). If you are born again, you are *in* the Spirit. That's a positional truth. But you might not be walking *after* the Spirit. You might be walking after the flesh and letting yourself be dominated by your physical senses—carnal mindedness (Rom. 8:6). A person like that won't experience the victory that's theirs in the Spirit.

If you aren't born again, you are *in* the flesh. That's your position. But you could walk *after* the Spirit. In other words, you could imitate the things of the Spirit. Although you could do some right things, it won't change your standing with God.

It also won't change your sin nature. Only being born again can do that.

How can you tell if you're walking after the Spirit or after the flesh? Well, what are your thoughts focused on? Are they on the flesh? Is your mind occupied with fear, strife, depression, or poverty? If so, you're after the flesh.

If you're after the Spirit, you'll be thinking about God. You'll be meditating on His Word and who you are in Christ. You'll have perfect peace, because your mind is stayed on Him (Is. 26:3). It's really that simple!

Spirit Minded

For to be carnally minded is *death; but to be spiritually minded* is *life and peace.*

Romans 8:6

The word *carnal* is related to the Spanish word *carne*.[3] You may have eaten or heard of the Spanish dish *chili con carne*, which just means "chili with meat." So, in other words, if you are carnally minded, you're being a meathead! In other words, you're just thinking according to your flesh.

For instance, if someone treats you badly, and you mull it over again and again, you'll be hurt, depressed, and offended. That's what carnal-mindedness produces—death. It's not so much what that person did to you that made you angry, bitter, and upset. It's what you meditated and thought about that empowered it in your life.

When I was younger, I was ready to fight at the drop of a hat, *and I would have been the one to drop the hat!* My friend Joe Nay once gave me a word, saying that he saw me like a runner on a racetrack. I was ahead of the pack, but the people who were watching were telling me I was doing it all wrong.

Joe said I went into the grandstands to argue with those people. He said, "If you do that, you may win the argument, but you'll lose the race." That really blessed me, and I ended up getting to the place where I just trusted God to handle those things while I focused on what He called me to do.

Years ago, there was a minister who got up in front of their people and criticized my ministry. Among other things, they said that I was "the slickest cult since Jim Jones" and encouraged people to burn my materials. For those of you who don't remember Jim Jones, he was a preacher who convinced his church to sell everything they owned, build a commune in the jungles of South America, and eventually commit mass suicide. So, that was quite an accusation to make!

I don't know exactly why they said those things, and I could have responded by defending myself, but I was just so secure in my relationship with God that I didn't give it any more thought. As a matter of fact, when this same minister sent out a letter requesting finances for a project, we sent them money. I just continued being a blessing to them.

About twenty years later, we were scheduled as guests on the same television show. In the green room, they told me how much they enjoyed my *Gospel Truth* program and loved our ministry. We ended up exchanging phone numbers, and since then, we've had meals together. It was just awesome how the Lord repaired our relationship.

It's not what people do to you that makes you angry but how you think *about* it. If you're carnally minded, you'll get death. If you're spiritually minded, you'll get life and peace.

Believe and Confess

For with the heart man believeth unto righteousness; and with the mouth confession is made unto salvation. For the scripture saith, Whosoever believeth on him shall not be ashamed.

Romans 10:10–11

Salvation isn't based on living holy. It's based on heart belief and mouth confession (Rom. 10:9), which is much more than just saying some words. It's talking about a firm commitment, a complete reliance, and an absolute trust in Jesus Christ as your Lord and Master. You're dependent on Him for salvation.

Many folks simply won't believe that faith in Jesus alone produces salvation. They believe that they must also be holy. But, as we've seen, that's not what Paul was saying. As I stated before, salvation is not about saying some special words. It's believing with your heart *and* confessing with your mouth.

During meetings, ministers may give an invitation for people to receive salvation. In response, many people repeat what's popularly known as "The Sinner's Prayer." But in some cases, people just mouth the words religiously. It's not coming from a sincere heart of faith.

First, you believe it in your heart; then you speak it with your mouth. It's a combination of the two. When you truly believe from your heart, God will never disappoint you. He's faithful. If you confess with your mouth and believe in your heart, you will be saved.

That isn't talking only about the initial born-again experience. It also means everything that comes as a result of what

Jesus Christ did—healing, deliverance, and prosperity—is available to you in the same way you received Him (Col. 2:6).

If you need healing in your body, all you have to do is confess with your mouth and believe in your heart, and according to the Bible, you'll be healed. You see, the Gospel is specifically referring to grace as the means by which we have access to salvation, healing, deliverance, and all the things of God.

"Salvation," like the word "Gospel," has also become a religious cliché. People have diminished and changed what salvation really means. To the average religious person, salvation means the forgiveness of your sins, being born again, or going to heaven. Now, it includes those things, but it's not limited to that.

The root of the Greek word translated "*salvation*" is σώζω ("*sōzō*").[4] While it is often translated "save," it is also translated "made whole" in reference to physical healing in Matthew 9:22, Mark 5:34, and Luke 8:48. In James 5:15, referring to a sick person, it says, "*the prayer of faith shall save the sick,*" and "*if he have committed sins, they shall be forgiven him.*"

Salvation applies to healing. It applies to deliverance. It applies to forgiveness of sins and everything else Jesus made available through the atonement, taking the sins of the whole world into His own body on the cross (1 Pet. 2:24). Salvation is a package deal, and it's up to you to believe it and receive it!

Conclusion

The Gospel is the power of God that releases the effects of salvation in our lives. Salvation is much more than just being born again. It refers to every benefit that the believer is entitled to through Jesus. Therefore, if we are not experiencing the abundance that Jesus provided for us—in any area of our lives—then we are having a problem understanding and believing the Gospel.

It took me over twenty years to learn the things I've shared with you in this booklet. They have revolutionized my life and are some of the most profound things anyone could understand.

The truths found in the book of Romans are as pertinent today as they were when Paul wrote them. Our current religious system causes people to trust in their own goodness and performance for right relationship with God.

We can never be good enough to have God owe us right standing. He has to give it to us as a gift. Nobody is good enough to earn relationship with God through their performance. The fact that people are trusting in their own performance is the very reason why Satan is able to defeat them.

Are you struggling with depression, discouragement, or other problems, even though you're born again? You may have asked the Lord into your heart, and you know you're saved, but you haven't seen yourself dead to sin, sickness, and poverty. You still see yourself as a sinner, sick, and poor.

If you're basing God's acceptance on any of your actions, then you aren't believing the Gospel. That's the very reason so many people are frustrated today. They aren't enjoying the peace and victory God brings. They haven't understood that salvation is a gift. Instead of trying so hard, we just need to give up, raise the white flag of surrender, and start trusting in God's grace.

FURTHER STUDY

If you enjoyed this booklet and would like to learn more about some of the things I've shared, I suggest my teachings:

- *Romans: Paul's Masterpiece on Grace*
- *Galatians*
- *Hebrews: Living in the New Covenant Reality*
- *Discover the Keys to Staying Full of God*
- *The Old Man is Dead*

Plus 200,000 hours of free teaching on our website.

These teachings are available for free at **awmi.net** or can be purchased at **awmi.net/store**.

Go deeper in your relationship with God by browsing all of Andrew's free teachings.

Receive Jesus as Your Savior

Choosing to receive Jesus Christ as your Lord and Savior is the most important decision you'll ever make!

God's Word promises, *"That if thou shalt confess with thy mouth the Lord Jesus, and shalt believe in thine heart that God hath raised him from the dead, thou shalt be saved. For with the heart man believeth unto righteousness; and with the mouth confession is made unto salvation"* (Rom. 10:9–10). *"For whosoever shall call upon the name of the Lord shall be saved"* (Rom. 10:13). By His grace, God has already done everything to provide salvation. Your part is simply to believe and receive.

Pray out loud: "Jesus, I acknowledge that I've sinned and need to receive what you did for the forgiveness of my sins. I confess that You are my Lord and Savior. I believe in my heart that God raised You from the dead. By faith in Your Word, I receive salvation now. Thank You for saving me."

The very moment you commit your life to Jesus Christ, the truth of His Word instantly comes to pass in your spirit. Now that you're born again, there's a brand-new you!

Please contact us and let us know that you've prayed to receive Jesus as your Savior. We'd like to send you some free materials to help you on your new journey. Call our Helpline: **719-635-1111** (available 24 hours a day, seven days a week) to speak to a staff member who is here to help you understand and grow in your new relationship with the Lord.

Welcome to your new life!

Receive the Holy Spirit

As His child, your loving heavenly Father wants to give you the supernatural power you need to live a new life. *"For every one that asketh receiveth; and he that seeketh findeth; and to him that knocketh it shall be opened...how much more shall* your *heavenly Father give the Holy Spirit to them that ask him?"* (Luke 11:10–13).

All you have to do is ask, believe, and receive! Pray this: "Father, I recognize my need for Your power to live a new life. Please fill me with Your Holy Spirit. By faith, I receive it right now. Thank You for baptizing me. Holy Spirit, You are welcome in my life."

Some syllables from a language you don't recognize will rise up from your heart to your mouth (1 Cor. 14:14). As you speak them out loud by faith, you're releasing God's power from within and building yourself up in the spirit (1 Cor. 14:4). You can do this whenever and wherever you like.

It doesn't really matter whether you felt anything or not when you prayed to receive the Lord and His Spirit. If you believed in your heart that you received, then God's Word promises you did. *"Therefore I say unto you, What things soever ye desire, when ye pray, believe that ye receive* them, *and ye shall have* them" (Mark 11:24). God always honors His Word—believe it!

We would like to rejoice with you, pray with you, and answer any questions to help you understand more fully what has taken place in your life!

Please contact us to let us know that you've prayed to be filled with the Holy Spirit and to request the book *The New You & the Holy Spirit.* This book will explain in more detail about the benefits of being filled with the Holy Spirit and speaking in tongues. Call our Helpline: **719-635-1111** (available 24 hours a day, seven days a week).

Notes

1. *Blue Letter Bible*, s.v. "μεταμορφόω" ("metamorphoō"). Accessed January 14, 2025, https://www.blueletterbible. org/lexicon/g3339/kjv/tr/0-1/

2. *American Heritage Dictionary*, s.v. "condemn," accessed January 14, 2025, https://ahdictionary.com/word/ search.html?q=condemn

3. *SpanishDictionary.com*, s.v. "carne," accessed January 14, 2025, https://www.spanishdict.com/translate/carne

4. *Blue Letter Bible*, s.v. "sōtēría" ("σωτηρία"), accessed January 9, 2025, https://www.blueletterbible.org/ lexicon/g4991/kjv/tr/0-1/, *Blue Letter Bible*, s.v. "sōtér" ("σωτήρ"), accessed January 9, 2025, https://www. blueletterbible.org/lexicon/g4990/kjv/tr/0-1/, and *Blue Letter Bible*, s.v. "sṓzō" ("σώζω"), accessed January 9, 2025, https://www.blueletterbible.org/lexicon/g4982/ kjv/tr/0-1/

Call for Prayer

If you need prayer for any reason, you can call our Helpline, 24 hours a day, seven days a week at **719-635-1111**. A trained prayer minister will answer your call and pray with you.

Every day, we receive testimonies of healings and other miracles from our Helpline, and we are ministering God's nearly-too-good-to-be-true message of the Gospel to more people than ever. So, I encourage you to call today!

About the Author

Andrew Wommack's life was forever changed the moment he encountered the supernatural love of God on March 23, 1968. As a renowned Bible teacher and author, Andrew has made it his mission to change the way the world sees God.

Andrew's vision is to go as far and deep with the Gospel as possible. His message goes far through the *Gospel Truth* television program, which is available to over half the world's population. The message goes deep through discipleship at Charis Bible College, headquartered in Woodland Park, Colorado. Founded in 1994, Charis has campuses across the United States and around the globe.

Andrew also has an extensive library of teaching materials in print, audio, and video. More than 200,000 hours of free teachings can be accessed at **awmi.net**.

Contact Information

Andrew Wommack Ministries, Inc.

PO Box 3333
Colorado Springs, CO 80934-3333
info@awmi.net
awmi.net

Helpline: 719-635-1111 (available 24/7)

Charis Bible College

info@charisbiblecollege.org
844-360-9577
CharisBibleCollege.org

For a complete list of all of our offices,
visit **awmi.net/contact-us**.

Connect with us on social media.

Andrew Wommack's

LIVING COMMENTARY
DIGITAL STUDY BIBLE

Andrew Wommack's *Living Commentary* digital study Bible is a user-friendly, downloadable program. It's like reading the Bible with Andrew at your side, sharing his revelation with you verse by verse.

Main features:
- Bible study software with a grace-and-faith perspective
- Over 27,000 notes by Andrew on verses from Genesis through Revelation
- *Adam Clarke's Commentary on the Bible*
- *Albert Barnes' Notes on the Whole Bible*
- *Matthew Henry's Concise Commentary*
- 12 Bible versions
- 3 optional premium translation add-ons: *New Living Translation*, *New International Version*, and *The Message* (additional purchase of $9.99 each)
- 2 concordances: *Englishman's Concordance* and *Strong's Concordance*
- 2 dictionaries: *Collaborative International Dictionary* and *Holman's Dictionary*
- Atlas with biblical maps
- Bible and *Living Commentary* statistics
- Quick navigation, including history of verses
- Robust search capabilities (for the Bible and Andrew's notes)
- "Living" (i.e., constantly updated and expanding)
- Ability to create personal notes
- Accessible online and offline

Whether you're new to studying the Bible or a seasoned Bible scholar, you'll gain a deeper revelation of the Word from a grace-and-faith perspective.

Purchase Andrew's *Living Commentary* today at **awmi.net/living** and grow in the Word with Andrew.

Item code: 8350

ANDREW WOMMACK MINISTRIES